Dr. E. Marcel Jones

Hunger

21 Principles Of Success For People Who Crave Greatness In Life

ISBN: 9798852052971

HUNGER
21 Principles Of Success For People Crave Greatness In Life

Published by Verse One Enterprises
An imprint of E. Marcel Ministries

www.emarceljones.com

<u>Special Thanks</u>

To God be the glory for sharing the vision for <u>HUNGER</u>. I'm grateful for my supportive wife, children, and family for inspiring me to reach for GREATNESS every morning. A shout out to my incredible *Cummings Street Church* family and staff for challenging me to be 1% GREATER each day. And, blessings to K. Gillespie and J. Hunter for your encouragement while completing this writing project.

Introduction

Are you hungry for greatness? Do you crave being great or at least better than average at what you do? Do you have an insatiable appetite to be the best? Do you want to greatly impact the lives of those connected to you?

Perhaps your desire is to be a great parent, a great supervisor, a great leader, a great friend, a great lover, a great spouse, a great athlete, a great performer, a great teacher, a great employee, or a great person!

For the average person reading this book, greatness will not be passed along by some GREAT distant relative or fall from a GREAT raincloud. Instead, the greatness you desire must be cultivated, nurtured, grown from within until it manifests externally for the world to witness. For the majority of us, greatness is a hunger that must be fed daily. We must feed our potential with life-giving words and actions that create momentum. In fact, greatness will require a tenacity and faith that can only be birthed from deep within your very soul.

The road to greatness is long, difficult, dangerous, and challenging. But, the reward will be worth the struggle. If you're ready to take this journey, follow along as we reveal 21 principles for achieving and maintaining the greatness you desire in life.

Learn how to break through limitations and barriers, and discover what it takes to take your life to the next level. Come along this journey toward becoming 1% GREATER each day.

HOW TO USE

Designate a quiet space and some uninterrupted time each week to read one principle. Afterwards, flip over to _Applying The Principle_ and complete each of the questions. This section is designed to challenge your thinking around the implementation of each principle. At the end of the week, make certain that you return to the _Grows, Goals, and Gratitude_ section for the greatest amount of impact.

Applying The Principle
How often is this principle applied to your life?

(Circle the progression graphic below that best fits)

1%	25%	50%	75%	100%
Rarely	Occasionally	Regularly	Frequently	Consistently

What new habits could you implement that would help manifest this principle, daily?

_____

How different would your life be if you were able to consistently apply this particular principle to your life?

_____

What hindrances or obstacles can you identify that are preventing you from reaching the optimal level?

_____

What immediate steps could you make today that would start you on the path to becoming a better version of yourself?

_____

HOW TO USE

At the end of the week, make certain that you return to the *Grows, Goals, and Gratitude* section for the greatest amount of impact and to maximize use of each principle.

GROWS,   GOALS,   & GRATITUDE
Self-Reflection

GROWS
This week, I've grown in the following ways:

_____

_____

_____

GOALS
I will work on achieving each of the goals listed below:

1._____

2._____

3._____

GRATITUDE
All is not perfect, but I'm grateful for:

_____

_____

_____

_____

Table of Contents

The Principle of Investment
You get out of it what you put into it

I recall when I first opened my first savings account as a teenager. My father instructed me to put a percentage of my weekly earnings from my part-time job at *Sears Department Store* into my new savings account. Every week, he would remind me, "Don't spend all your money, son." Even then, he was teaching me the vital lesson of saving a portion of what I earn.

So, I did just that! I saved a little, and Lord knows that I also spent a lot of what I was earning every week. Until one day, I realized that my spending was far exceeding my saving. I was wasting more money than I was putting aside. It even got to the point when I started pulling from my savings just to handle my weekly obligations. By the end of the year, my savings was in the red. I had nothing to show for all the long hours of work that I had put in to my job. You will discover that the time, money, love, dedication, and energy you put into your endeavors will pay huge dividends.

The **Principle of Investment** can also be applied to your relationships. Relationships feed off of what you invest into them. When it comes to your goals and career aspirations, this principle rings loud and clear. You can't expect a rich salary and great career, if you don't invest the commitment and time that success needs to sustain it. In fact, you even can apply this principle to your health. Because our bodies feed off what we put into them, the end result will always be the same – we will always get out of them what we put into them.

Applying The Principle of Investment

How often is this principle applied to your life?

(Circle the progression graphic below that best fits)

1%	25%	50%	75%	100%
Rarely	Occasionally	Regularly	Frequently	Consistently

What new habits could you implement that would help manifest this principle, daily?

_____

_____

_____

How different would your life be if you were able to consistently apply this particular principle to your life?

_____

_____

_____

What hindrances or obstacles can you identify that are preventing you from reaching the optimal level?

_____

_____

_____

What immediate steps could you make today that would start you on the path to becoming a better version of yourself?

_____

_____

_____

GROWS, GOALS, & GRATITUDE
This Week's Self-Reflection

GROWS
This week, I've grown in the following ways:

_____
_____
_____
_____
_____
_____

GOALS
I will work on achieving each of the goals listed below:

1._____
2._____
3._____
4._____
5._____
6._____
7._____

GRATITUDE
All is not perfect, but in this moment, I'm grateful for:

_____
_____
_____
_____
_____
_____
_____
_____

Principle of Hope

Avoid negative thinking and separate from negative people

Nothing kills HOPE quicker than negative thinking. And, nothing can destroy the very essence of HOPE completely more than negative people. It is imperative that you carefully choose the company that you keep and as much as possible refuse to buy into the negative thoughts that may enter your mind occasionally. Because, negativity is toxic to a healthy relationship.

The **Principle of Hope** helps to bring positive expectations to your life and encourages you to engage in activities that produce joy. The principle encourages us to focus on the present moment and manifest meaningful experiences, daily. By using this principle, your creativity and drive will be fueled, creating a positive future for you and those around you. Hope teaches us to find joy in every day experiences and stay in tune with our source of belief in order to accelerate the process of creating the future you desire.

By applying this principle to your life, you will remain focused on the present while maintaining a positive outlook for the future. You'll be mindful of your thoughts and remain in this state, even when things don't go as planned. In addition, you will recognize the importance of embracing all the experiences in life — both the good and the bad. And, you'll learn to appreciate your beliefs regardless to what obstacles and hindrances surface along the way. Maintaining hope will enable you to appreciate the beauty in life and focus on the positive aspects of every situation.

Applying The Principle of Hope

How often is this principle applied to your life?

(Circle the progression graphic below that best fits)

1%	25%	50%	75%	100%
Rarely	Occasionally	Regularly	Frequently	Consistently

What new habits could you implement that would help manifest this principle, daily?

_____
_____
_____

How different would your life be if you were able to consistently apply this particular principle to your life?

_____
_____
_____

What hindrances or obstacles can you identify that are preventing you from reaching the optimal level?

_____
_____
_____

What immediate steps could you make today that would start you on the path to becoming a better version of yourself?

_____
_____
_____

GROWS, GOALS, & GRATITUDE
This Week's Self-Reflection

GROWS
This week, I've grown in the following ways:

_____
_____
_____
_____
_____
_____

GOALS
I will work on achieving each of the goals listed below:

1._____
2._____
3._____
4._____
5._____
6._____
7._____

GRATITUDE
All is not perfect, but I'm grateful for:

_____
_____
_____
_____
_____
_____
_____
_____

The Principle Connectivity
Seek people who energize you—not those who deplete you

People you choose to connect with will make the biggest impact on the direction your life takes. If you connect with folks who leave you drained and depleted, your life's journey will likely be lackluster, unfulfilling, and taxing. However, should you choose to connect with others who have just as much to offer as you have, the power that comes from that type of association could quite possibly open doors of opportunity that you never imagined.

Don't worry so much about AMPS and WATTAGE, when it comes to **The Principle of Connectivity**. Connectivity is all about your willingness to remain plugged into a source of power. The principle is an incredibly important element in life because it seeks to foster collaboration and connection with those around you. When you apply this principle to your life, your reach and sphere of influence increases.

Your connections must be intentional. Connecting with persons who are compatible with your dreams and goals builds your network of support. These connections depend on solid relationships. In order to take the action steps required, you must identify several strategies for staying connected.

One way to connect with the right people is to express your appreciation for them. Everyone welcomes a compliment, and that conversation can lead to a connection. Or, perhaps you could attend some of the community events in your area and network with the movers and shakers in your city. Be prepared to highlight what you do well so that the connection appears mutually beneficial. The *Principle of Connectivity* is all about fostering lifelong connections and collaborating with those around you.

Applying The Principle of Connectivity
How often is this principle applied to your life?

(Circle the progression graphic below that best fits)

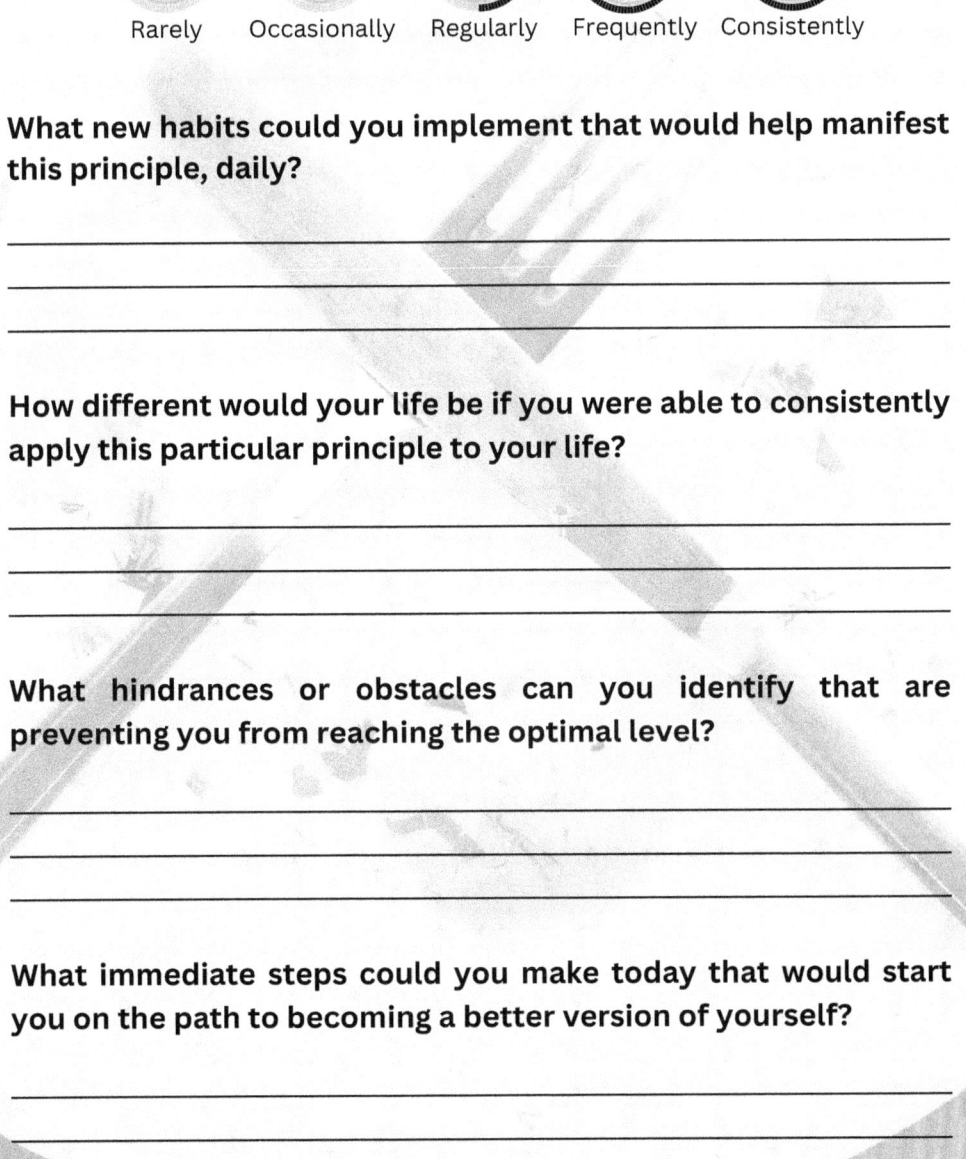

| 1% | 25% | 50% | 75% | 100% |
| Rarely | Occasionally | Regularly | Frequently | Consistently |

What new habits could you implement that would help manifest this principle, daily?

_____

_____

_____

How different would your life be if you were able to consistently apply this particular principle to your life?

_____

_____

_____

What hindrances or obstacles can you identify that are preventing you from reaching the optimal level?

_____

_____

_____

What immediate steps could you make today that would start you on the path to becoming a better version of yourself?

_____

_____

_____

GROWS, GOALS, & GRATITUDE
This Week's Self-Reflection

GROWS
This week, I've grown in the following ways:

_____
_____
_____
_____
_____
_____

GOALS
I will work on achieving each of the goals listed below:

1._____
2._____
3._____
4._____
5._____
6._____
7._____

GRATITUDE
All is not perfect, but I'm grateful for:

_____
_____
_____
_____
_____
_____
_____

Principle of Growth
Challenge what hinders you & push through what prevents you

How much have you grown in the past year? What about in the past 5 or 10 years? I know it may be hard to measure yourself against yourself, and you may not notice much of a change. But, the truth is either you're growing or dying. No one is really completely stagnant. Just take a look at every aspect of your life and ask yourself the question, "Have I grown in any of these areas in the last five years?"

Socially, Mentally, Physically, Financially, Spiritually

Environment and nutrients are the key to producing growth in these areas. The wrong soil content, wrong climate, or wrong amount of nourishment can kill your growth. It is vital that you acknowledge how much you influence your own potential. YOU are the one that can make the most meaningful changes to your life. If you want to grow in any of the areas listed above, it's on YOU. You don't have to wait or rely on other factors or folks to make it happen. If you desire to grow, take the time to look inwardly and evaluate your motives, gifts, environment, and potential. Once you assess where you are, begin making small changes to your attitude and actions, making sure your purpose is aligned with your core values and beliefs. This will help you identify the additional steps you will need take in order to reach your goals and continue to grow.

It is important that YOU take responsibility for your own growth. YOU drive the process and control your destiny. You must be willing to take chances and accept constructive feedback in order to improve each day. By taking ownership of your own development, you can gain an understanding of how to improve and achieve the life that you desire.

Applying The Principle of Growth
How often is this principle applied to your life?

(Circle the progression graphic below that best fits)

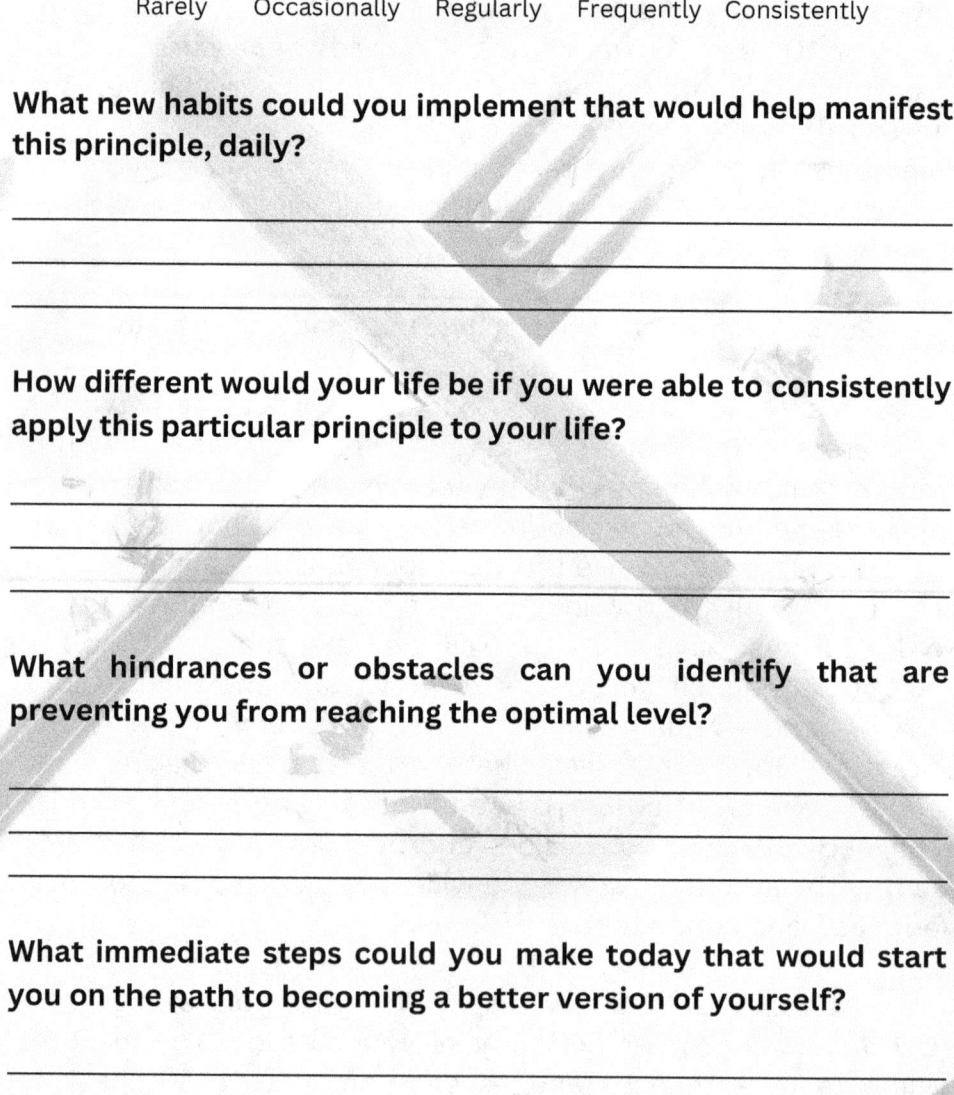

1%	25%	50%	75%	100%
Rarely	Occasionally	Regularly	Frequently	Consistently

What new habits could you implement that would help manifest this principle, daily?

_____

_____

_____

How different would your life be if you were able to consistently apply this particular principle to your life?

_____

_____

_____

What hindrances or obstacles can you identify that are preventing you from reaching the optimal level?

_____

_____

_____

What immediate steps could you make today that would start you on the path to becoming a better version of yourself?

_____

_____

_____

GROWS, GOALS, & GRATITUDE
This Week's Self-Reflection

GROWS
This week, I've grown in the following ways:

_____
_____
_____
_____
_____
_____

GOALS
I will work on achieving each of the goals listed below:

1._____
2._____
3._____
4._____
5._____
6._____
7._____

GRATITUDE
All is not perfect, but I'm grateful for:

_____
_____
_____
_____
_____
_____
_____
_____

<u>The Principle of Learning</u>

Find the lesson in every situation and learn from it

Are you a lifelong learner? Or, did learning cease for you once you left high school? I have earned three degrees but have never stopped learning. The **Principle of Learning** encourages you to never stop gaining knowledge. In fact, it encourages you to seek knowledge daily and to never assume that you know everything. No matter how much you have learned, there is always more to learn.

By taking the initiative to seek new knowledge, you will constantly stimulate your dendrites and brain cells. Applying this principal daily will keep your mind engaged. The result can lead to acquiring valuable skills and life experiences which can extend far beyond any knowledge you can find in books or classrooms.

The *Principle of Learning* helps you to stay curious and remain willing to try new things. It is a great way to assist you in developing a new mindset to address old problems and to have a positive attitude towards failure. Sometimes, the best lessons are those we learn from past failures. We learn what not to do and occasionally discover newer more innovative approaches that we never would have considered before.

Since even our mistakes can produce learning tools, there is really no need to become discouraged when we fail. Instead, we should embrace the challenge of learning and learn to relish in our successes. The *Principle of Learning* can also help you to maximize your potential, which could result in greater opportunities, a more positive outlook on life, and a healthier self-image.

Applying The Principle of Learning

How often is this principle applied to your life?

(Circle the progression graphic below that best fits)

1%	25%	50%	75%	100%
Rarely	Occasionally	Regularly	Frequently	Consistently

What new habits could you implement that would help manifest this principle, daily?

_____

_____

_____

How different would your life be if you were able to consistently apply this particular principle to your life?

_____

_____

_____

What hindrances or obstacles can you identify that are preventing you from reaching the optimal level?

_____

_____

_____

What immediate steps could you make today that would start you on the path to becoming a better version of yourself?

_____

_____

_____

GROWS, GOALS, & GRATITUDE
This Week's Self-Reflection

GROWS
This week, I've grown in the following ways:

_____
_____
_____
_____
_____
_____

GOALS
I will work on achieving each of the goals listed below:

1._____
2._____
3._____
4._____
5._____
6._____
7._____

GRATITUDE
All is not perfect, but I'm grateful for:

_____
_____
_____
_____
_____
_____
_____

Principle of Pursuit

Pursue the vision, accomplish the goal, and proclaim the win

What are you pursuing in life? Is it peace? Fame? Wealth? Health? What gets you up in the morning and starts your chase? What motivates you to keep going despite obstacles and detours in your life? Whatever you're pursuing, keep chasing after it until it becomes your reality. I encourage you to adopt a newer approach to living and begin eating, sleeping, and dreaming your pursuits and passions until you obtain what you are pursuing.

The **Principle of Pursuit** encourages us to set personal goals and remain determined to achieve them. You can apply this principle by striving to do the things that will make your life better. When you have a goal in mind, you can use the Principle of Pursuit to motivate yourself to take action towards that goal.

In order to accomplish your goals, it is important to take small steps towards your objective. Learn to pursue tasks daily by breaking down projects into smaller, more manageable chunks that can help guide you towards the direction you are headed. Taking the time to break down big projects into smaller ones can help you remain organized and focused.

Finally, as you pursue your goals, it is important to remember that obstacles and failures are a part of the process. The *Principle of Pursuit* teaches us that failure is a learning experience and that we should use these moments in our lives to grow and become better versions of ourselves.

What are your plans? What is your purpose? What are your pursuits? Unite your plans, purposes, and pursuits today, and tomorrow, hit the ground running and chasing after what life has to offer.

Applying The Principle of Pursuit

How often is this principle applied to your life?

(Circle the progression graphic below that best fits)

1%	25%	50%	75%	100%
Rarely	Occasionally	Regularly	Frequently	Consistently

What new habits could you implement that would help manifest this principle, daily?

_____

_____

_____

How different would your life be if you were able to consistently apply this particular principle to your life?

_____

_____

_____

What hindrances or obstacles can you identify that are preventing you from reaching the optimal level?

_____

_____

_____

What immediate steps could you make today that would start you on the path to becoming a better version of yourself?

_____

_____

_____

GROWS, GOALS, & GRATITUDE
This Week's Self-Reflection

GROWS
This week, I've grown in the following ways:

_____
_____
_____
_____
_____
_____
_____

GOALS
I will work on achieving each of the goals listed below:

1._____
2._____
3._____
4._____
5._____
6._____
7._____

GRATITUDE
All is not perfect, but I'm grateful for:

_____
_____
_____
_____
_____
_____
_____
_____
_____

The Principle of Foundation
Continually build on a solid foundation

The most important section of your life's structure is its foundation. Because, if your foundation is not stable, everything you place on top of it will be in jeopardy of crumbling. Sure, you might be able to accomplish a few things, initially, due to a shaky foundation. But, soon, you'll learn to invest your time and energies into shifting and adjusting what you're attempting to construct in life. You'll learn the value of spending time on securing your foundation or your core.

The **Principle of Foundation** is all about achieving long-term goals through small, sustainable changes and realizing that few things can be built to last without first laying a proper foundation. Applying this to your life means being mindful of the present moment and understanding how your *current* decisions can affect your future state of being.

Every decision you make must be in alignment with your foundational values and goals. Everything must fall in line with this concept. Otherwise, even the slightest move or most minor decision can threaten the entire structure and integrity of what you're attempting to build. The key is to set realistic and achievable, short-term goals that eventually prosper into larger manifestations.

You can initiate and sustain this principle by developing a daily practice or routine. It could be something as simple as carving out a few minutes to read, meditate, or practice gratitude. Or, perhaps you're attempting to reset your health but starting out the day with a brisk walk or change in your morning diet. Either way, setting aside a small amount of time each day to focus on your goals will eventually lead to long-term success and a more stable foundation.

Applying The Principle of Foundation

How often is this principle applied to your life?

(Circle the progression graphic below that best fits)

1%	25%	50%	75%	100%
Rarely	Occasionally	Regularly	Frequently	Consistently

What new habits could you implement that would help manifest this principle, daily?

_____

_____

_____

How different would your life be if you were able to consistently apply this particular principle to your life?

_____

_____

_____

What hindrances or obstacles can you identify that are preventing you from reaching the optimal level?

_____

_____

_____

What immediate steps could you make today that would start you on the path to becoming a better version of yourself?

_____

_____

_____

GROWS, GOALS, & GRATITUDE
This Week's Self-Reflection

GROWS
This week, I've grown in the following ways:

_____
_____
_____
_____
_____
_____

GOALS
I will work on achieving each of the goals listed below:

1._____
2._____
3._____
4._____
5._____
6._____
7._____

GRATITUDE
All is not perfect, but I'm grateful for:

_____
_____
_____
_____
_____
_____
_____

Principle of Responsibility

Own what you are responsible for, admit your errors, and move forward.

All of us have some level of responsibility. I don't care if you are a child or an elderly adult. ALL of us are responsible for something or someone, if nothing more than our own lives. As such, the worst thing we can do with our responsibility is to refuse ownership.

The **Principle of Responsibility** empowers us to take charge of our own development. The principle charges you to hold yourself accountable for your actions. It dismisses the opportunity to find a scapegoat or excuse ownership for failures and mishaps. Instead, it places the onus directly on the shoulders of the individual with the greatest amount of control - YOU. If you desire to live a more balanced and purposeful life, it begins with accepting responsibility for the outcome of your decisions.

When you're applying the *Principle of Responsibility*, you have to be aware of your thoughts, beliefs, motives, fears, and behaviors. This is the beginning of taking proper ownership of your situation. Thinking about how your decisions will affect your well-being and impact the lives of others is of paramount importance. Master this and you'll master the art of positive decision-making.

When you develop a greater sense of self-awareness and take responsibility for your actions, it allows you to critically evaluate your choices and assess any hidden motives. By doing this, you will have more control over your decisions and life, and ultimately manifest the life and success you desire.

Applying The Principle of Responsibility

How often is this principle applied to your life?

(Circle the progression graphic below that best fits)

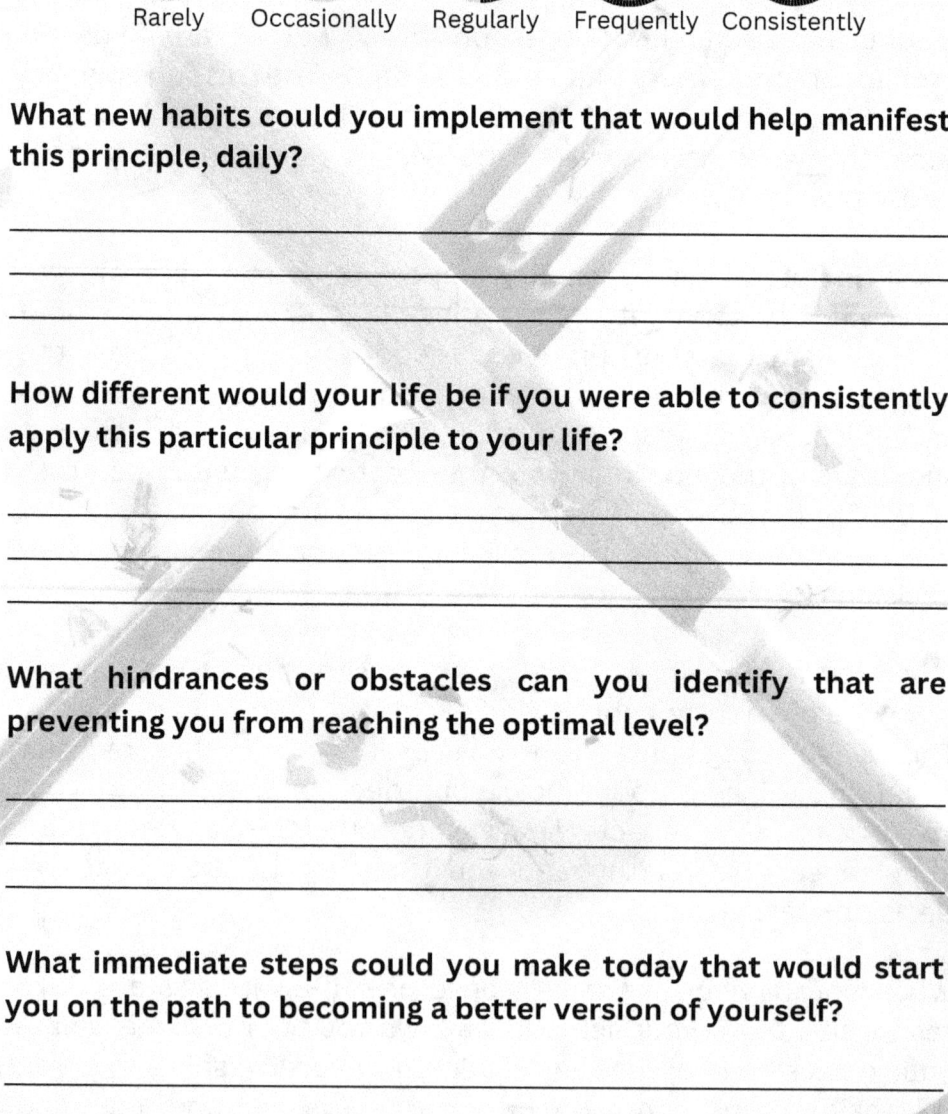

1%	25%	50%	75%	100%
Rarely	Occasionally	Regularly	Frequently	Consistently

What new habits could you implement that would help manifest this principle, daily?

_____

_____

_____

How different would your life be if you were able to consistently apply this particular principle to your life?

_____

_____

_____

What hindrances or obstacles can you identify that are preventing you from reaching the optimal level?

_____

_____

_____

What immediate steps could you make today that would start you on the path to becoming a better version of yourself?

_____

_____

_____

GROWS, GOALS, & GRATITUDE
This Week's Self-Reflection

GROWS
This week, I've grown in the following ways:

_____
_____
_____
_____
_____
_____

GOALS
I will work on achieving each of the goals listed below:

1._____
2._____
3._____
4._____
5._____
6._____
7._____

GRATITUDE
All is not perfect, but I'm grateful for:

_____
_____
_____
_____
_____
_____
_____

The Principle of Focus
Spotlight your goals; laser your strategies

Spotlights are for theater stages, security alerts, or to call *Batman* into action in Gotham City. But, **lasers** are for intricate activities such as surgical procedures that require focus. Focus is essential for the anyone who desires to reach his or her goals and succeed in life. Utilizing the **Principle of Focus** can help you stay organized and stay on track with your aspirations.

Every area of your life requires focus. Thus, the *Principle of Focus* should be used to establish goals, first. Never set out to accomplish anything without first becoming like a laser and focusing in on specific goals. If you are a leader in your household or within your community, you should focus on setting attainable and meaningful goals that will result in positive changes in your life and will help progress those around you to the next level.

You must have a plan in place that includes realistic deadlines that you can commit to and remain focused on for a set period of time. One important way to use focus is to identify what tasks are *essential* for you to complete and then prioritize these accordingly. This type of focus will enable you to determine what's doable today and what can wait for another day.

Maintaining your focus can also help you divide and conquer daily tasks. By dividing your goals into smaller tasks, you can focus on one goal at a time which will improve the chances of you succeeding in each task.

The *Principle of Focus* manifests self-discipline as well. It encourages self-determination and self-control. Disciplining yourself gives you a competitive edge over others who lack this essential character trait. If you are determined to succeed in every area of your life, it is essential that you remain focused.

Applying The Principle of Focus

How often is this principle applied to your life?

(Circle the progression graphic below that best fits)

1%	25%	50%	75%	100%
Rarely	Occasionally	Regularly	Frequently	Consistently

What new habits could you implement that would help manifest this principle, daily?

_____

_____

_____

How different would your life be if you were able to consistently apply this particular principle to your life?

_____

_____

_____

What hindrances or obstacles can you identify that are preventing you from reaching the optimal level?

_____

_____

_____

What immediate steps could you make today that would start you on the path to becoming a better version of yourself?

_____

_____

_____

GROWS, GOALS, & GRATITUDE
This Week's Self-Reflection

GROWS
This week, I've grown in the following ways:

_____
_____
_____
_____
_____
_____

GOALS
I will work on achieving each of the goals listed below:

1._____
2._____
3._____
4._____
5._____
6._____
7._____

GRATITUDE
All is not perfect, but I'm grateful for:

_____
_____
_____
_____
_____
_____
_____

Principle of Self-Care

There's only one YOU: Take care of your mind, body, and soul

When is the last time you took some time for YOU? I mean, when is the last time you treated yourself to your favorite meal, your favorite activity, or your favorite hangout spot? The **Principle of Self-Care** is the idea that we are responsible for taking care of ourselves to the best of our ability. It is not your spouse's responsibility or your employer's responsibility — but YOUR responsibility. This principle stresses the importance of making healthy choices in life. If applied appropriately, it will help you maintain a balanced and stable life, improve your overall well-being, and increase your satisfaction with life.

Initially, your first step is to assess your individual needs. You should identify which areas of your life are *most important* and determine which specific actions will help you improve or maintain your well-being in those areas. Make note of any physical, mental, emotional, social, and spiritual needs. Be certain to include the amount of time you wish to dedicate to daily activities such as work, rest, play, relationships, and other interests.

Next, develop a plan of action. Include strategies you could employ that would help you fulfill those things you desire, such as dieting, exercising, stress and time management, and even spiritual development.

Last, create an environment that will support your self-care. It's vital that you remove or reduce all stressors such as toxic relationships and create opportunities to practice self-care activities instead. Monitor your emotional and spiritual well-being regularly and adjust as necessary. Your quality of life will thank you later.

Applying The Principle of Self-Care

How often is this principle applied to your life?

(Circle the progression graphic below that best fits)

1%	25%	50%	75%	100%
Rarely	Occasionally	Regularly	Frequently	Consistently

What new habits could you implement that would help manifest this principle, daily?

_____

_____

_____

How different would your life be if you were able to consistently apply this particular principle to your life?

_____

_____

_____

What hindrances or obstacles can you identify that are preventing you from reaching the optimal level?

_____

_____

_____

What immediate steps could you make today that would start you on the path to becoming a better version of yourself?

_____

_____

_____

GROWS,   GOALS,   & GRATITUDE
This Week's Self-Reflection

GROWS
This week, I've grown in the following ways:

_____
_____
_____
_____
_____
_____

GOALS
I will work on achieving each of the goals listed below:

1._____
2._____
3._____
4._____
5._____
6._____
7._____

GRATITUDE
All is not perfect, but I'm grateful for:

_____
_____
_____
_____
_____
_____
_____
_____

The Principle of Gratitude

Value the things you own, the people you know, and the moments you experience

Gratitude extends well beyond Thanksgiving Day. But, gratitude is a daily practice of recognizing that as bad as things might be right now, within you is a spirit of thankfulness that all hope is not lost. Applying the **Principle of Gratitude** to your life is a great way to become a more content and more optimistic person.

When you are gracious, you exhibit an attitude that allows you to be thankful for all the good things in your life. You're able to concentrate on those things you have that are positive and wholesome and the experiences that you have been blessed to encounter. The principle can be a powerful tool for self-improvement, helping you to take a step back from your daily life and take in the beauty of the moment. Applying this principle has both mental and physical benefits, including increased feelings of contentment and happiness and reduced anxiety and stress.

Practicing gratitude is not complicated but can easily become part of your daily routine during moments of prayer and self-reflection. Begin by recording seven (7) things that you are grateful for each morning. This practice keeps appreciation for life at the top of your mind. Even throughout the day as you think of other things you are grateful for, try putting the language of gratitude into practice by making it part of your daily conversations.

Take time each day to appreciate the world around you and the people in your life. Then, sit back and watch how life will begin to take on a different landscape. Your entire narrative can change with just a minute of gratitude.

Applying <u>The Principle of Gratitude</u>

How often is this principle applied to your life?

(Circle the progression graphic below that best fits)

1%	25%	50%	75%	100%
Rarely	Occasionally	Regularly	Frequently	Consistently

What new habits could you implement that would help manifest this principle, daily?

_____

_____

_____

How different would your life be if you were able to consistently apply this particular principle to your life?

_____

_____

_____

What hindrances or obstacles can you identify that are preventing you from reaching the optimal level?

_____

_____

_____

What immediate steps could you make today that would start you on the path to becoming a better version of yourself?

_____

_____

_____

GROWS, GOALS, & GRATITUDE
This Week's Self-Reflection

GROWS
This week, I've grown in the following ways:

_____
_____
_____
_____
_____
_____

GOALS
I will work on achieving each of the goals listed below:

1._____
2._____
3._____
4._____
5._____
6._____
7._____

GRATITUDE
All is not perfect, but I'm grateful for:

_____
_____
_____
_____
_____
_____
_____

Principle of Kindness

At the end of each day, make sure you have practiced kindness and esteemed the worth of others

As a little boy, I was taught to hold the door open for women and elderly people. It's a practice that has become so routine that I do it automatically without giving any thought to it. So much about the way I communicate, serve, and even care for my own family is rooted in the **Principle of Kindness**.

A famous quote emerged from the movie ***The Help***, "You is smart; You is kind; You is important." In other words, kindness along with intelligence and self-worth is an asset to be desired. A little kindness goes a great distance. The *Principle of Kindness* seeks to encourage us to practice civility. It could be in the way you treat others or just in the words you choose to deliver as you interact with people.

Being courteous, polite, and respectful means you are exercising understanding and patience, even in difficult situations. Being kind is deliberate and intentional. There will be times when opportunities to display kindness may not be apparent. But, just know that the world we live in has plenty of room for good will. Whether you're donating cans to a food drive, checking on a friend in need, or volunteering at a unhoused shelter, acts of kindness take nothing away from the initiate but provides a wealth of love to the recipient.

Practicing both internal and external benevolence is the key to upholding the *Principle of Kindness*. Remember to speak kindly to others and spread mercy throughout the day. The person or persons on the receiving end may or may not express gratitude, but don't allow their disregard affect your gentleness. Your motive is not to gain their gratitude but to share your kindness.

Applying The Principle of Kindness

How often is this principle applied to your life?

(Circle the progression graphic below that best fits)

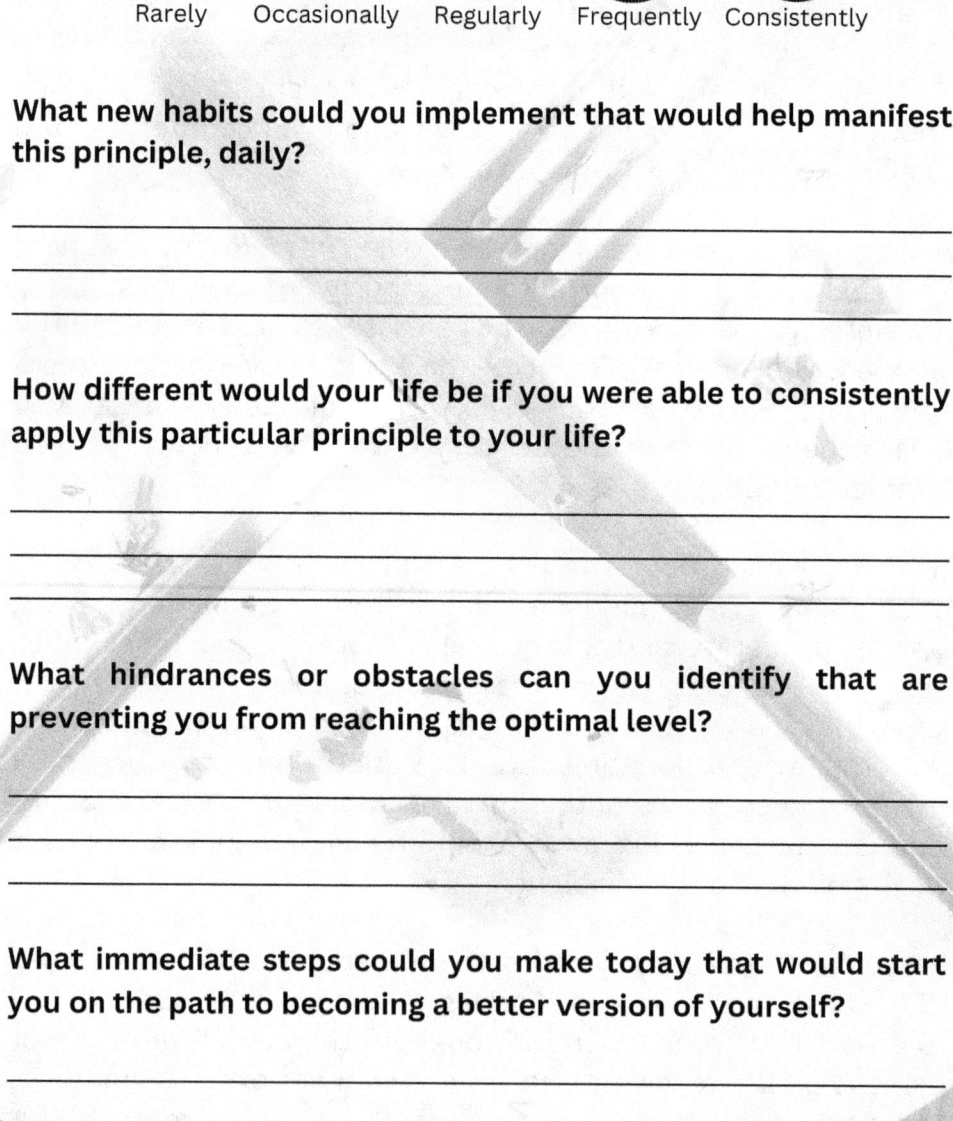

| 1% | 25% | 50% | 75% | 100% |
| Rarely | Occasionally | Regularly | Frequently | Consistently |

What new habits could you implement that would help manifest this principle, daily?

_____

_____

_____

How different would your life be if you were able to consistently apply this particular principle to your life?

_____

_____

_____

What hindrances or obstacles can you identify that are preventing you from reaching the optimal level?

_____

_____

_____

What immediate steps could you make today that would start you on the path to becoming a better version of yourself?

_____

_____

_____

GROWS, GOALS, & GRATITUDE
This Week's Self-Reflection

GROWS
This week, I've grown in the following ways:

_____
_____
_____
_____
_____
_____

GOALS
I will work on achieving each of the goals listed below:

1._____
2._____
3._____
4._____
5._____
6._____
7._____

GRATITUDE
All is not perfect, but I'm grateful for:

_____
_____
_____
_____
_____
_____
_____

Principle of Control

Our external response is often symptomatic of our own internal struggles

I recall sitting in Dr. Logan's 6th grade classroom and enduring the constant belittling coming from the mouth of a fellow student in the class. I had endured all I could take. So, before I knew it, I had jumped to my feet and was punching the student as hard as I could. I had lost control.

The **Principle of Control** endeavors to help men create a better and more stable lifestyle. The idea is to take control of your life by taking responsibility for your own decisions, thoughts, and actions. This begins by identifying the things in your life that you want to better control. It might include your spending habits, your physical health, your emotional stability, your career path, or even the quality of your relationships with others. Knowing what you can control gives you a sense of reality and reduces your stress factors.

Next, be willing to take responsibility for the decisions you make because YOU are in the driver's seat and your hands are on the wheel. So, embrace any mistakes and celebrate all your wins. This allows you to have a greater understanding of your actions and how they impact your life and the people around you.

Know your limits and strive to become the best version of yourself because, after all, you are in control. When you know your limits, it keeps you from exceeding your capabilities. When you have realistic expectations, you are less likely to become overwhelmed and are able to focus on the things you can control. Take control of your own destiny and makes things happen.

<u>Applying The Principle of Control</u>
How often is this principle applied to your life?

(Circle the progression graphic below that best fits)

1%	25%	50%	75%	100%
Rarely	Occasionally	Regularly	Frequently	Consistently

What new habits could you implement that would help manifest this principle, daily?

_____

_____

_____

How different would your life be if you were able to consistently apply this particular principle to your life?

_____

_____

_____

What hindrances or obstacles can you identify that are preventing you from reaching the optimal level?

_____

_____

_____

What immediate steps could you make today that would start you on the path to becoming a better version of yourself?

_____

_____

_____

GROWS, GOALS, & GRATITUDE
This Week's Self-Reflection

GROWS
This week, I've grown in the following ways:

_____
_____
_____
_____
_____
_____

GOALS
I will work on achieving each of the goals listed below:

1._____
2._____
3._____
4._____
5._____
6._____
7._____

GRATITUDE
All is not perfect, but I'm grateful for:

_____
_____
_____
_____
_____
_____
_____

The Principle of Voice
You have a voice — find it and use it

During my first year of teaching, the stress and strain on my vocal cords created a raspy, hoarse tone in my voice. It made it difficult for me to teach, maintain discipline, and even to be understood. I had to find alternative ways of communicating.

The **Principle of Voice** values interpersonal communication. It involves speaking up, asserting yourself, and expressing your opinions, needs, and feelings. This principle is a way of being assertive and allowing yourself to be heard.

There are several ways to apply this principle in your everyday life. Initially, you should be aware of your own feelings. It can be difficult to express yourself if you are constantly feeling overwhelmed or threatened. So, taking a moment to acknowledge this feeling will enable you to use your voice appropriately.

As you find your voice, learn to use it calmly and directly. It is important to be clear in what you are saying and why you are saying it so that others won't misunderstand you.

Remember to take responsibility for the words you use and the tone in which it is spoken. It is important to be aware of how your words can impact others. Make no apologies for using your voice. Always take responsibility for what flows from your tongue. By applying the *Principle of Voice*, you can become more confident in expressing yourself and be better equipped to engage in effective interpersonal communication.

Applying The Principle of Voice

How often is this principle applied to your life?

(Circle the progression graphic below that best fits)

1%	25%	50%	75%	100%
Rarely	Occasionally	Regularly	Frequently	Consistently

What new habits could you implement that would help manifest this principle, daily?

_____

_____

_____

How different would your life be if you were able to consistently apply this particular principle to your life?

_____

_____

_____

What hindrances or obstacles can you identify that are preventing you from reaching the optimal level?

_____

_____

_____

What immediate steps could you make today that would start you on the path to becoming a better version of yourself?

_____

_____

_____

GROWS, GOALS, & GRATITUDE
This Week's Self-Reflection

GROWS
This week, I've grown in the following ways:

_____
_____
_____
_____
_____
_____

GOALS
I will work on achieving each of the goals listed below:

1. _____
2. _____
3. _____
4. _____
5. _____
6. _____
7. _____

GRATITUDE
All is not perfect, but I'm grateful for:

_____
_____
_____
_____
_____
_____
_____

The Principle of Financial Stewardship
Save wisely, spend wisely, and share wisely

One of the best lessons my parents instilled in me was to work hard for what I wanted and save a portion of what I earn. This lesson is foundational to the **Principle of Financial Stewardship**. Everyone needs a spending plan that adheres closely to the tenants of financial stewardship. These tenants include the practice of *planning, monitoring,* and *managing* your wealth in order to ensure financial security and success for both the present and the future.

Applying this principle to your daily life can help you make the most of your money and create a healthier financial future. In fact, when it comes to financial stewardship, one of the most important things you can do is to create a ***budget***. A budget will help you keep track of your income and spending habits. Additionally, it will help you decide which expenses are necessary and which are not vital to daily living. Once you have established a budget, it is important to *monitor* your finances and make any adjustments as needed.

Another way to practice financial stewardship is to *save* a portion of your income regularly. Maintaining a savings account can help ensure that you have access to money in the future. Saving even a small amount each week or every month can provide revenue for unexpected expenses, vacations, or large purchases.

When it comes to credit, the *Principle of Financial Stewardship* encourages responsible and proper use. Having good credit is important for making big purchases in the future. So, to ensure that your credit is in good standing, be sure to pay your bills on time and limit the amount you charge to credit cards each month. By utilizing the *principles of financial stewardship,* you can create a secure a healthy future and enjoy a lifetime of financial success.

Applying The Principle of Financial Stewardship

How often is this principle applied to your life?

(Circle the progression graphic below that best fits)

1%	25%	50%	75%	100%
Rarely	Occasionally	Regularly	Frequently	Consistently

What new habits could you implement that would help manifest this principle, daily?

_____

_____

_____

How different would your life be if you were able to consistently apply this particular principle to your life?

_____

_____

_____

What hindrances or obstacles can you identify that are preventing you from reaching the optimal level?

_____

_____

_____

What immediate steps could you make today that would start you on the path to becoming a better version of yourself?

_____

_____

_____

GROWS, GOALS, & GRATITUDE
This Week's Self-Reflection

GROWS
This week, I've grown in the following ways:

_____
_____
_____
_____
_____
_____

GOALS
I will work on achieving each of the goals listed below:

1._____
2._____
3._____
4._____
5._____
6._____
7._____

GRATITUDE
All is not perfect, but I'm grateful for:

_____
_____
_____
_____
_____
_____
_____

The Principle of Discipline

Discipline is the STICKTUITIVENESS you need to be successful

The **Principle of Discipline** is an incredibly important concept for achieving success in life. When you implement this principle into your everyday life, the results can be invaluable in establishing winning patterns and reaching life goals. There are essentially four ways to apply this principle to your life.

The initial step involves *establishing a routine* to encourage self-discipline. Setting regular times for waking, exercising, meditating, eating, working, and even leisure time can help create healthy habits that will ensure productivity and satisfaction throughout the day.

Next, try *staying organized* and making discipline a priority in your life. This means clearing your life of the clutter that leads to stress. This move will free your thoughts and provide you with greater satisfaction since now you'll be able to complete those daily tasks that have been mounting.

Thirdly, the *Principle of Discipline* requires us to *follow through with our goals*. Be certain that you evaluate your short-term goals on a regular basis and make plans to achieve long-term goals regularly.

If you take this principle seriously, it can serve as a powerful tool for creating success and efficiency in your life. Take the time to establish routines, stay organized, manage your emotions, set appropriate goals, and watch your daily life transform!

Applying The Principle of Discipline
How often is this principle applied to your life?

(Circle the progression graphic below that best fits)

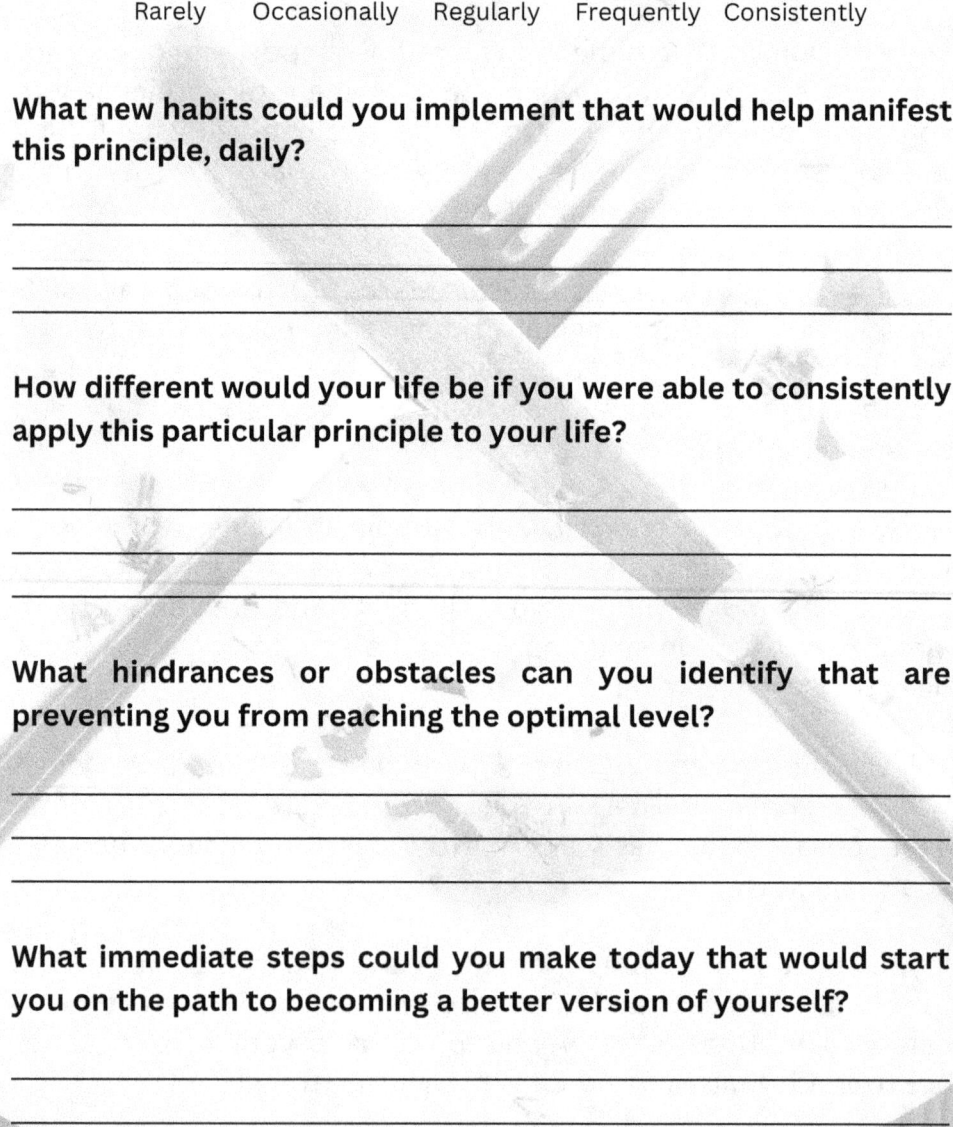

1%	25%	50%	75%	100%
Rarely	Occasionally	Regularly	Frequently	Consistently

What new habits could you implement that would help manifest this principle, daily?

_____

_____

_____

How different would your life be if you were able to consistently apply this particular principle to your life?

_____

_____

_____

What hindrances or obstacles can you identify that are preventing you from reaching the optimal level?

_____

_____

_____

What immediate steps could you make today that would start you on the path to becoming a better version of yourself?

_____

_____

_____

GROWS, GOALS, & GRATITUDE
This Week's Self-Reflection

GROWS
This week, I've grown in the following ways:

_____

_____

_____

_____

_____

_____

GOALS
I will work on achieving each of the goals listed below:

1._____

2._____

3._____

4._____

5._____

6._____

7._____

GRATITUDE
All is not perfect, but I'm grateful for:

_____

_____

_____

_____

_____

_____

The Principle of Confrontation
Face what intimidates you — You can't change what you're unwilling to face

The **Principle of Confrontation** is an important life skill that can help you navigate difficult situations and relationship conflicts. It encourages us to be honest and direct about our thoughts and feelings and to confront others in a thoughtful, intentional, and respectful manner.

When you apply this principle to your life, you are more likely to take a proactive approach to managing conflicts. This, in turn, should create more positive outcomes. Those of use who embrace this principle tend to be clear and concise about our feelings and are more likely to listen and respond without overreacting.

The *Principle of Confrontation* is useful for effectively addressing personal relationships, but it can also be applied to professional conflicts. When conflicts are confronted properly in the workplace, disputes are more likely to be resolved peacefully. This result may be due to the presence of open dialogue and empathy for the other person. It's a win-win for all parties involved when the situation is approached with diplomacy.

When we address our concerns head on and engage in open dialogue with those we have conflict with, the likelihood of a resolution or reconciliation is high. It can be a great way to guarantee a meaningful and positive relationship personally or professionally. In fact, your peers will learn to appreciate your approach to communicating with them in times of conflict. And, your family will regard you as a trustworthy member of the household and one that they can trust with their emotions and opinions.

Applying The Principle of Confrontation
How often is this principle applied to your life?

(Circle the progression graphic below that best fits)

1%	25%	50%	75%	100%
Rarely	Occasionally	Regularly	Frequently	Consistently

What new habits could you implement that would help manifest this principle, daily?

_____

_____

_____

How different would your life be if you were able to consistently apply this particular principle to your life?

_____

_____

_____

What hindrances or obstacles can you identify that are preventing you from reaching the optimal level?

_____

_____

_____

What immediate steps could you make today that would start you on the path to becoming a better version of yourself?

_____

_____

_____

GROWS, GOALS, & GRATITUDE
This Week's Self-Reflection

GROWS
This week, I've grown in the following ways:

_____
_____
_____
_____
_____
_____

GOALS
I will work on achieving each of the goals listed below:

1._____
2._____
3._____
4._____
5._____
6._____
7._____

GRATITUDE
All is not perfect, but I'm grateful for:

_____
_____
_____
_____
_____
_____
_____

Principle of Discretion

Keep your plans and pursuits to yourself — Release them only when you're ready to birth them

The **Principle of Discretion** operates under the assumption that we choose to exercise good judgement, especially when deciding whether to share information or take action. When this principle is put into practice, it allows for greater control over conversations and interactions with others. The *Principle of Discretion* provides a more ethical approach to making decisions as well.

Before you initiate or engage in a conversation around a sensitive topic, consider when and how you should choose to share information. Both when you share information and how you share information is critical. Using discretion when talking to colleagues, friends, complete strangers, or even family members is wise.

It's always best to limit the amount of information you share in order to ensure that your conversation remains productive and respectful. For folks you don't know well, it's always a good practice to limit how much information you share and to monitor the tone used to deliver information. Try waiting until all the facts are known before passing judgement on a situation. Discretion in this regard allows you to make decisions based on the facts at hand rather than emotionally responding.

Once you make a decision to share, what you share should remain consistent so that all parties involved know what to expect. Also, be certain you are transparent about the reasoning behind your decision to share. This will help build and maintain trust and foster better relationships with others.

Applying The Principle of Discretion

How often is this principle applied to your life?

(Circle the progression graphic below that best fits)

1%	25%	50%	75%	100%
Rarely	Occasionally	Regularly	Frequently	Consistently

What new habits could you implement that would help manifest this principle, daily?

_____

_____

_____

How different would your life be if you were able to consistently apply this particular principle to your life?

_____

_____

_____

What hindrances or obstacles can you identify that are preventing you from reaching the optimal level?

_____

_____

_____

What immediate steps could you make today that would start you on the path to becoming a better version of yourself?

_____

_____

_____

GROWS, GOALS, & GRATITUDE
This Week's Self-Reflection

GROWS
This week, I've grown in the following ways:

_____
_____
_____
_____
_____
_____

GOALS
I will work on achieving each of the goals listed below:

1._____
2._____
3._____
4._____
5._____
6._____
7._____

GRATITUDE
All is not perfect, but I'm grateful for:

_____
_____
_____
_____
_____
_____
_____

The Principle of Character

Your character will take you places that your talent cannot

We are often judged by not only our exterior presentation but also by the content of our character. The **Principle of Character** encourages integrity at the highest level. The idea is to exhibit an authentic and meaningful profile that is honest, respectful, and self-disciplined. It's your character that's on display, daily.

As you interact with others, remember to treat everyone with kindness and honor their opinions. This speaks to your character. No matter how different others might be, you must be a person of character that consistently practices respect and integrity. Strive to show that your words and actions match by behaving in a manner that is consistent with your core beliefs.

Create healthy environments where everyone can grow together. This will speak to your genuine and loving character. Strive to go out of your way to make sure that everyone feels respected, supported, and heard. This will speak to the genuineness of your character.

In your work setting, display hard work, focus, and dedication so that peers and supervisors witness the tenacity of your character. Keep organized, work diligently, and be willing to put in the extra effort, even if others don't do the same. Make every effort to get to know your coworkers and build strong relationships based on trust and honesty.

Ultimately, by implementing the *Principle of Character*, you will begin living an authentic and honest life. And, others will recognize the realness of your spirit and appreciate the transparency of your character.

Applying The Principle of Character

How often is this principle applied to your life?

(Circle the progression graphic below that best fits)

1%	25%	50%	75%	100%
Rarely	Occasionally	Regularly	Frequently	Consistently

What new habits could you implement that would help manifest this principle, daily?

_____

_____

_____

How different would your life be if you were able to consistently apply this particular principle to your life?

_____

_____

_____

What hindrances or obstacles can you identify that are preventing you from reaching the optimal level?

_____

_____

_____

What immediate steps could you make today that would start you on the path to becoming a better version of yourself?

_____

_____

GROWS, GOALS, & GRATITUDE
This Week's Self-Reflection

GROWS
This week, I've grown in the following ways:

_____
_____
_____
_____
_____
_____

GOALS
I will work on achieving each of the goals listed below:

1._____
2._____
3._____
4._____
5._____
6._____
7._____

GRATITUDE
All is not perfect, but I'm grateful for:

_____
_____
_____
_____
_____
_____
_____

Principle of Forgiveness

Forgiveness is as much for you as it is for others

The **Principle of Forgiveness** can be life-changing and liberating. Forgiveness is more beneficial to the person harboring resentment and bitterness than it is for the offender(s). When we take the time to practice forgiveness, we open ourselves to greater happiness and harmony.

Try applying the *Principle of Forgiveness* to your daily life when someone wrongs you or offends you. Take the time to reflect and forgive them by releasing the hurt instead of holding onto to negative thoughts or feelings about the person. Even if forgiving them is difficult, it is important to forgive those who have hurt you. It does not mean you are condoning their behavior but simply releasing yourself from the pain and resentment you are feeling. This, in turn, creates the space you need to heal in your heart.

Also, recognize the importance of being kind and forgiving to yourself. Self-forgiveness is a vital step towards healing, especially when you've harbored hatred or resentment toward yourself. Try journaling or writing a simple letter to yourself regarding the incident or situation. Reflect on what happened, then tell yourself to forgive, and let it go! Self-forgiveness is a key component in your journey to self-awareness. So, take time to reflect and allow yourself to forgive any of your actions or feelings that you may have harbored guilt or resentment over.

Refuse to dwell on the wrongs done to you. If someone has offended you, it can be easy to slip into a pattern of bitterness. So, practicing the *Principle of Forgiveness* allows you to break free of the past and focus on the beauty of the present moment. Open yourself up to a greater sense of peace and well-being.

Applying The Principle of Forgiveness

How often is this principle applied to your life?

(Circle the progression graphic below that best fits)

1%	25%	50%	75%	100%
Rarely	Occasionally	Regularly	Frequently	Consistently

What new habits could you implement that would help manifest this principle, daily?

_____

_____

_____

How different would your life be if you were able to consistently apply this particular principle to your life?

_____

_____

_____

What hindrances or obstacles can you identify that are preventing you from reaching the optimal level?

_____

_____

_____

What immediate steps could you make today that would start you on the path to becoming a better version of yourself?

_____

_____

_____

GROWS, GOALS, & GRATITUDE
This Week's Self-Reflection

GROWS
This week, I've grown in the following ways:

_____
_____
_____
_____
_____
_____

GOALS
I will work on achieving each of the goals listed below:

1._____
2._____
3._____
4._____
5._____
6._____
7._____

GRATITUDE
All is not perfect, but I'm grateful for:

_____
_____
_____
_____
_____
_____
_____
_____

The Principle of Greatness
Learn to be great on purpose

If you want to be great, you have to be intentional. The **Principle of Greatness** encourages those of us who desire to be exceptional to incorporate a few strategies into our daily living.

Begin by striving to do the best job you possibly can when completing task, chores, or assignments. When you take the extra step to do something the right way instead of taking the easy way out, the benefit positively impacts the world around you. Doing your best also sets an example for others in your circle and can give you a sense of pride and accomplishment.

Another way to apply this principle is to always be open to learning. When you are constantly seeking out new knowledge and striving to improve yourself, this continuous action can create countless opportunities for growth. You'll discover that the knowledge gained from being a life-long learner will provide you with a wealth of wisdom to share with others.

Be certain that you set optimistic and achievable goals as well. This will increase your outlook on life and the things you are accomplishing. Having a positive attitude and believing that you can accomplish great things will help you stay motivated and will attract like-minded people.

Consider practicing a small act of kindness every day. Whether it's a smile, a kind word, or just taking the time to listen to someone's needs, an act of kindness can have positive and long-lasting benefits. It can also make you feel fulfilled and connected to the power of God. Others will look upon you as a person of greatness and you will have impacted their life in a great way.

Applying The Principle of Greatness
How often is this principle applied to your life?

(Circle the progression graphic below that best fits)

1%	25%	50%	75%	100%
Rarely	Occasionally	Regularly	Frequently	Consistently

What new habits could you implement that would help manifest this principle, daily?

_____
_____
_____

How different would your life be if you were able to consistently apply this particular principle to your life?

_____
_____
_____

What hindrances or obstacles can you identify that are preventing you from reaching the optimal level?

_____
_____
_____

What immediate steps could you make today that would start you on the path to becoming a better version of yourself?

_____
_____
_____

GROWS, GOALS, & GRATITUDE
This Week's Self-Reflection

GROWS
This week, I've grown in the following ways:

_____

_____

_____

_____

_____

_____

GOALS
I will work on achieving each of the goals listed below:

1._____

2._____

3._____

4._____

5._____

6._____

7._____

GRATITUDE
All is not perfect, but I'm grateful for:

_____

_____

_____

_____

_____

_____

_____

For more great inspiration
Check out Dr. E. Marcel Jones' website
www.emarceljones.com